Jackie

2014

We'll Be Friends Through Thick & Thin

Celebrating the blessings of laughter and friendship

Love Ya,
Donna

Inspired by Faith

We'll Be Freinds Through Thick & Thin
ISBN 978-0-9895802-2-9

Published by Product Concept Mfg., Inc.
2175 N. Academy Circle #200, Colorado Springs, CO 80909

©2013 Product Concept Mfg., Inc. All rights reserved.

Written and Compiled by N. L. Roloff
in association with Product Concept Mfg., Inc.

All scripture quotations are from the King James version
of the Bible unless otherwise noted.

Scriptures taken from the Holy Bible,
New International Version®, NIV®.
Copyright © 1973, 1978, 1984 by Biblica, Inc.™
Used by permission of Zondervan.
All rights reserved worldwide.
www.zondervan.com

Sayings not having a credit listed are contributed by writers
for Product Concept Mfg., Inc. or in a rare case,
the author is unknown.

We'll Be Friends Through Thick & Thin

Friendship is a word the very sight
  of which in print makes the heart warm.

Augustine Birrell

$\mathcal{W}$hen we think of our friends, our closest and most special ones, our hearts warm, our step gets lighter and we feel ourselves smiling. That's because friends make life so much better than it would be without them. A life without friends would be like a world without sunshine, ice cream, shoe sales, laughter...the list goes on and on!

But what is it that we cherish most about our friends? The first thing that comes to mind is the comfort we get just from knowing we have someone to trust, rely on, share with, talk to and simply go through life with... someone who enriches our lives just by being in the world...someone we love who loves us back.

It's our best friends we can call in the middle of the night, who we can laugh with when we've done something silly, who believe in us even when we mess up, who have seen us at our worst as well as our best, and who love us anyway.

The value of friends has been recognized and celebrated for as long as mankind has existed and realized that life is much better shared than spent alone. And it's a truth we recognize and celebrate every day whenever we exchange a phone call or e-mail, spend an afternoon shopping or talking or just hanging out.

There are so many qualities that endear another person to us and earn them a special place in our hearts. It's hard to count them all. Just what is a friend anyway? It's definitely a subject worth exploring!

Friends Are a Blessing

Friends are kisses blown to us by angels.
Author Unknown

This is my commandment,
that ye love one another
as I have loved you.
John 15:12

Sometimes guardian angels are
right here by our side on earth,
helping us in times of trouble,
soothing us when we need comfort,
and giving us good advice when
we're about to make a big mistake.
They're called friends.

A true friend is the greatest of all blessings.
La Rochefoucauld

When I count my blessings,
I always count my friends first.
Author Unknown

Blessed are they who have the gift
of making friends, for it is one of God's best gifts.
It involves many things, but above all,
the power of going out of one's self,
and appreciating whatever is
noble and loving in another.
Thomas Hughes

Blessed is the influence of one true,
loving human soul on another.
George Eliot

The most heavenly moments are spent
enjoying laughter, life and love
with a very special friend.

GOD'S SPECIAL GIFT

God couldn't be everywhere,
and so He made friends...
He made them so we could have
someone to laugh with us,
and to cry with us,
Someone we could confide in
and know our secrets would be safe,
Someone we could tell our dreams to
and feel believed in.
He made friends so there would be someone
to share the good times with us
and to give us comfort and support
during the challenging times.
He made friends to understand our needs,
even when we have trouble
expressing them,
and to get our jokes even when
we mess up the punch lines,
but especially, God made friends
so we wouldn't have to eat
those great big ol' desserts
all by ourselves.

Friends Make Us Feel Loved

When you're having a hard day but you
don't want to admit it, and you're presenting
a smiling face to the world when you really
feel like crying, a friend will wait for a private
moment, take your hand and say
"Now tell me all about it…."

In meeting again after a separation,
acquaintances ask after our outward life,
friends after our inner life.
Marie von Ebner-Eschenbach

"Stay" is a charming word in a friend's vocabulary.
Louisa May Alcott

Friends are those rare people who ask how you are
and then wait for the answer.
Author Unknown

NO SPECIAL REASON

We all have cloudy days
when we feel a little down,
when there are way too many tasks
for us to do….
We feel we have too little
energy and time
to tackle every job and
see it through.

We sometimes ask ourselves
what life is all about,
if it's even worth the efforts
that we make…
the labor and the love
that we put in every deed
we do each day for
someone else's sake.

And then the sun breaks through—
a friend takes time to call,
no special reason,
Just to say "Hello"
that she was thinking of us,
and all we mean to her
and suddenly felt the need
to tell us so.

A true friend has a way of making
you feel like you are the only person
in the room and that just seeing you
has made their day brighter and better.

What is friendship?
It is loving companionship,
the nurturing of one life by another.

Love is a mighty power,
a great and complete good.
Love alone lightens every burden,
and makes the rough places smooth.

Thomas A Kempis

Friendship is the key that opens
the heart to life, to happiness, to sharing…
to feeling like you are loved
and have a place in the world.

Friends Stick with Us Through Thick and Thin

A TALE OF WOE

One day when I was young and fairly broke, I went to the public library to do some research for a writing assignment. When I came out, my old semi-broken down Dodge Polara was gone! It was only then that I noticed the sign that said "Tow Zone during Rush Hour, 4-6 PM."

In a panic, I called the police station and discovered that my car had been towed to their lot, that I had one hour to pick it up, and that I had to pay for it in cash. I needed the car to get to work the next day and I had only a few dollars in my purse—this was before ATMs. Things looked bad. I called my friend, Susie.

She listened sympathetically and said "I'll be right there to pick you up." I said I had no money and she said "Don't worry. I'll take care of it."

Good as her word, she arrived shortly in her equally beat-up car and got me to the tow lot just in time, where she lent me the money to bail out my car. She was a life-saver.

What I didn't find out about until later was this. When I called her, she was in the process of using a plunger on her overflowing toilet. And since she didn't have any cash either, she stopped by a bank and used a credit card, cash-advance check to get me the money to pay my ticket. She never said a word about any of this as she listened to my tale of woe.

Yes, Susie was a life-saver that day, when we were both much younger than we are today. We now live in different cities and haven't seen each other in years. But we always remember to call on each other's birthday and we talk for a long time, catching up on each other's lives. And we send each other e-mails we think the other would enjoy. She sends me funny pictures of her cats with hilarious captions. I send her pictures of my dog and my kids.

She was and is the best kind of friend. And I will always appreciate and love my dear friend, Susie.

We have been friends together
through sunshine and in shade.
Caroline Norton

Many friends will walk in
and out of your life,
but only true friends will leave
footprints in your heart.
Eleanor Roosevelt

Friends show their love in times of trouble,
not in happiness.
Euripedes

A friend loveth at all times.
Proverbs 17:17

He that is thy friend indeed
He will help thee in thy need.
William Shakespeare

The only way to have a friend
is to be one.
Ralph Waldo Emerson

A real friend never
gets in your way—
unless you happen to be
on the way down.
Author Unknown

In poverty and other
misfortunes of life,
true friends are a sure refuge.
Aristotle

May your right hand always
be stretched out in friendship,
and never in want.
Blessing

Misfortune shows those
who are not really friends.
Aristotle

When it seems like everyone else
is against you,
a true friend is for you.
And when no one has a good word
to say about you,
a friend will defend you,
And when no one else wants
to have anything to do with you,
a true friend is still there, by your side,
saying "Hey, it's good to see you.
Let's go get coffee!"

Hard times will always reveal true friends.
Proverb

Friendship isn't about who you've known
the longest. It's about who came and
never left your side.
Author Unknown

A friend is someone who,
when you've made a total fool
of yourself, thinks it's only
a temporary condition.
Author Unknown

When everyone has turned against you,
a true friend holds you up
and lets the world know she's on your side,
always has been...always will be...

Friends Have a Special Connection with Us that Time Only Strengthens

Sometimes you meet a person and it
seems like you've met before, even when you
know you haven't. There's an immediate comfort
in each other's company, a feeling of familiarity
that reaches out from one heart to the other,
as though you're recognizing an old friend.
And before you know it, the hours have
flown by as you discover all the reasons
you feel like you have known
each other forever.

Two may talk together under the same
roof for many years, yet never really meet;
and two others at first speech are old friends.
Mary Catherwood

Dear Friend,

Even if we haven't talked in days or seen each other in weeks, or even months, at the sound of your voice, time disappears. And before we know it, we're laughing at each other's jokes, encouraging each other's dreams and reminiscing about times we've shared. We're listening, really listening, to everything the other has to say about life, love, family, kids, pets, hopes, disappointments, the newest fashion purchase, the latest haircut, the best new recipe...any subject is worth discussing, every thought is worth sharing.

That's because we both know that between friends, there's an understanding and empathy that is always there, a constant interest in one another's life, feelings and thoughts...and a support for each other that only strengthens over time.

There's a special closeness that, at the sound of the other's voice, fills our hearts and makes us feel like it was only yesterday that we were last together.

Always set high value on
spontaneous kindness.
He whose inclination prompts him
to cultivate your friendship
of his own accord
will love you more than one
whom you have
been at pains to attach to you.
Samuel Johnson

Because you write to me often,
I thank you....
Never do I receive a letter from you,
but immediately we are together.
Seneca

Friends Can Always be Depended On

Marlene Dietrich once said that a friend is someone you can call at four in the morning. But then other people say a friend is someone who is considerate enough not to call you after 11:00 at night. I actually agree with both of them. A friend is someone with whom you have an understanding that it's okay to call at four in the morning if it's absolutely necessary but who usually will be more thoughtful and call before 11:00 at night. But you both know you can always depend on the other 24 hours a day, 7 days a week, for eternity, and if you need to call each other, then you just better do that, no matter what time of day it is. Because if you don't, your friend will say "Well, why in the world didn't you call me?!"

Friends are like stars.
You don't have to see them
to know that they are there.
Author Unknown

Walking with a friend in the dark
is better than walking alone in the light.
Helen Keller

It's hard to imagine this journey
without a good friend by my side.
A good friend is like the chocolate chips
in the trail mix of my life.

A friend in need is a friend indeed.
Proverb

A friend is someone who
doesn't check her calendar to see
if she has time for you...
instead she makes time for you.
Author Unknown

If you're alone, I'll be your shadow.
If you want to cry, I'll be your shoulder.
If you want a hug, I'll be your pillow.
If you need to be happy, I'll be your smile.
But any time you need a friend,
I'll just be me.
Author Unknown

Encourage one another
and build each other up.
I Thessalonians 5:11 NIV

Surely we ought to prize those
friends on whose principles and opinions
we may constantly rely—
of whom we may say in all emergencies,
"I know what they would think."
Hannah Farnham Lee

If a friend makes a promise,
she keeps it,
and if she's going to be late,
she calls,
and when it's your birthday,
she remembers,
and if something bad happens
in your life,
she checks to see if you're okay,
and when you say you're okay,
but you're really not,
she shows up with flowers
and a casserole,
so at least you don't have to cook
when you're feeling down.

Friends are like walls.
Sometimes you lean on them,
and sometimes it's enough
just to know they are there.
Author Unknown

Friends Believe in Us

Friends...
they cherish each other's hopes.
They are kind to each other's dreams.
Thoreau

In everyone's life, at some time,
our inner fire goes out. It is then burst
into flame by an encounter with another
human being. We should all be thankful for
those people who rekindle the inner spirit.
Albert Schweitzer

A friend is someone who knows the song in
your heart and can sing it back to you when
you have forgotten the words.
Author Unknown

Treat your friends as you do your pictures,
and place them in their best light.
Jennie Churchill

A friend is someone who doesn't
believe the gossip she hears about you
even if she knows it's true.
Author Unknown

A friend is someone who believes in you,
even when you don't believe in yourself.
Author Unknown

Live so that your friends can defend you,
but never have to.
Arnold Glasow

A friend is someone who listens to your dreams,
encourages you to believe in them,
does what she can to make them come true,
and then cheers the loudest
when you achieve success.

The glory of friendship is not the
outstretched hand, not the kindly smile,
nor the joy of companionship; it is the spiritual
inspiration that comes to one when you
discover that someone else believes in you
and is willing to trust you with a friendship.
Emerson

My best friend is the one
who brings out the best in me.
Henry Ford

Every once in a while,
we all need a little nudge,
just to remind us to get out of our rut,
dust off our dreams, and go out to face
the world. Dreams can get lost in the
hustle and bustle of every day life,
but a friend never forgets the hopes
in your heart, because she shares
them with you and wants to see you
reach the stars just to see
the smile on your face when you get there.

Friends Bring Out the Best in Us

"I can't do it," you say.
"You CAN do it," she says.
"I'm not good enough," you say.
"You are not only good enough...
you're the best," she says.
"I don't deserve it," you say.
"You do deserve it and more," she says.
"Maybe I can do it," you say.
"I know that you can," she says.
"Then I will try," you say.
"And I'll be there to help you,
in any way I can," she says.

A friend accepts us as we are yet helps
us to be all that we are capable of being.

Author Unknown

Even when we think
we can't go another step,
we can't change our lives or ourselves
and make a better life,
when we feel like everything
is stacked against us
and there's no hope,
a true friend cheers us on,
telling us we can do it,
we are better and stronger and smarter
than we ever imagined...
that we deserve more,
and that we will succeed.

As iron sharpens iron,
so one person sharpens another.
Proverbs 27:17 NIV

A real friend helps us think our best thoughts,
do our noblest deeds,
be our finest selves.
Author Unknown

A friend is, as it were, a second self.
Cicero

Friends Understand Us
Without Us Having to Say a Word

There is a golden thread that ties together
the hearts of true friends.
It is silent and invisible, yet full of meaning.
It floats in the air like a shaft of light
between two people,
and only those two people
can sense its presence and feel its warmth.
It is a wordless conversation filled with understanding
that comes from being connected
on the deepest level.

I always felt that the great high privilege,
relief and comfort of friendship was that
one had to explain nothing.
Katherine Mansfield

A friend knows what you're thinking
even if you don't say anything.
And she knows when you're upset
even if you say you're okay.
Because she doesn't need words
to feel what you're feeling
or to know what you mean.
She just knows.

The best kind of friend is one you
can sit on the porch with, never saying a word,
and walk away feeling like it was the best
conversation you've ever had.
Author Unknown

The language of friendship is not words,
but meanings.
Henry David Thoreau

Once in an age,
God sends to some of us a friend
who loves us...not the person we are,
but the angel we may be.
Harriet Beecher Stowe

Give me one friend, just one,
who meets the needs
of my varying moods.
Esther M. Clark

A friend can tell what you're thinking
just by looking at you,
and nods in understanding
before you say one word.

Friendship needs no words.
Dag Hammarskjold

Friends Make Life Worthwhile

My only sketch, profile,
of heaven is a large blue sky,
bluer and larger than the biggest
I have seen in June—
and in it are my friends—
every one of them.
Emily Dickinson

Friendship is the bread
of the heart.
Mary Mitford

My friends are my estate.
Emily Dickinson

I JUST HAD TO CALL YOU

It's lovely when life smiles on us
and things are going our way,
When the kids are being angels
and doing what we say.

It's so nice when that diet
we've struggled to stay on
Does just what it's supposed to
and those extra pounds are gone!

It's sweet when that new recipe
we've carefully put together
Emerges smelling heavenly
and then tastes even better!

All these things are nice but
something makes them much more fun—
it's calling up a friend,
a very special one…

And sharing all our stories
with somebody who cares,
and rejoices in our joys
just like they were theirs!

But friendship is precious,
not only in the shade but
in the sunshine of life,
and thanks to a benevolent
arrangement of things,
the greater part of life is sunshine.
Thomas Jefferson

A friend may well be reckoned
the masterpiece of nature.
Ralph Waldo Emerson

Do not protect yourself by a fence,
but rather by your friends.
Proverb

There is nothing on this earth
more to be prized
than true friendship.
Thomas Aquinas

Nothing but heaven
itself is better than a friend who
is really a friend.
Plautus

The world is round
so that friendship
may encircle it.
Pierre Teilhard de Chardin

I know not whether our names
will be immortal;
I am sure our friendship will.
Walter Savage Lander

PHONE CALL BETWEEN TWO LONG-TIME FRIENDS:

When people spend a lot of time together, they may begin to think alike—and even finish each other's sentences.

"Hey…"

"Lunch?"

"Love to! Where?"

"That place with those sesame thingees?"

"You mean the one with the brass doodads on the table?"

"Yeah, where we last ran into what's her name."

"Perfect! Fifteen minutes?"

"See ya there!"

It isn't so much what's
on the table that counts,
as what's on the chairs.
W. S. Gilbert

I have learned that to be
with those I like is enough.
Walt Whitman

The person who tries to live alone
will not succeed as a human being.
His heart withers if it does not answer
another heart. His mind shrinks away if he
hears only the echoes of his own thoughts
and finds no other inspiration.
Pearl S. Buck

Good friends often finish
each other's sentences. Really good friends help
finish each other's dessert.

I know what things are good: friendship
and work and conversation.
Rupert Brooke

Fortify yourself with a flock of friends!
You can select them at random,
write to one, dine with one, visit one,
or take your problems to one.
There is always at least one who
will understand, inspire,
and give you the lift you
may need at the time.
George Matthew Adams

Today when I woke up,
the sky looked gray and gloomy,
there were bills to pay and
chores that needed doing yesterday,
and people making demands on my time...
time that I didn't have.
And then I thought
of you and our plans to get together,
and in one instant,
everything seemed less overwhelming,
the day more promising,
and the world kinder...
just because you're in it!

Friendship is the only cement that will ever
hold the world together.
Woodrow Wilson

Friendship is like a house that has been
buffeted by winds and rain and time.
It stands strong and fast against
everything that batters it,
and though the worse for wear and,
perhaps less beautiful to the naked eye
than it once was, it survives...
and goes on to provide a place for us to go
where we are always welcome and safe.

Best friend, my wellspring
in the wilderness!
George Eliot

A hug is worth a thousand words.
A friend is worth more!
Charles Caleb Colton

Friends Love Us for Who We Are

WE'VE GOT EACH OTHER

My friend doesn't care if my outfits aren't chic
or if my nails haven't been "done,"
My friend doesn't care if I'm not a size 2
or I tell her a really bad pun.

My friend doesn't see that I'm getting more wrinkles
or that there's more gray in my hair,
And she couldn't care less that I'm sometimes forgetful
or that parts of me age here and there.

I guess that's because, when we get right down to it,
we've weathered a lot side-by-side.
Life is a journey that's much more rewarding
when a friend is along for the ride.

My friend cares about all the moments we've shared
how we try to be kind to each other,
She knows what matters isn't fortune or fame
but just that we've got one another.

It is one of the blessings
of old friends that you can afford
to be stupid with them.
Ralph Waldo Emerson

A true friend knows everything about you,
your quirks, your habits,
your unguarded self...
and likes you anyway!
Author Unknown

A friend is someone who
has seen you at your worst
and always remembers your best.

My friend is one...
who takes me for what I am.
Henry David Thoreau

'Tis the privilege of friendship to talk nonsense
and have that nonsense respected.
Charles Lamb

A true friend thinks you're a good egg,
even if you're half-cracked.
Author Unknown

A friend is someone who stands by you
when you make a mess of things,
does what she can do
to help you clean things up,
then assures you that this too shall pass
and things will be better tomorrow.

Friends Comfort Us

FRIENDS GET US THROUGH THE DAY

My friend is always there
with caring advice,
especially when I'm about
to do something impulsive
and crazy....

My friend always listens
when I just need to vent
but lets me know when
it's time "to let it go."

My friend has a way of knowing
when I'm thinking of her
and will call or email me
at the same time I call or email her.

My friend can always think
of something good about me
when I'm feeling really down
on my self.

My friend remembers little things
like I don't like anchovies
or pineapple or black olives on my pizza...
so she never orders them when we're together.

My friend always thinks of me
when she finishes a book or sees a movie
she knows I will like, and makes sure
I know about it so I can enjoy it, too.

My friend can make my heart melt
with a kind look or a reassuring touch
when I least expect it
but need it the most.

My friend...what would I ever do
without you and your smile and understanding
and the bright and beautiful light
you bring into my life?

Thank you for being in my life
and being my friend,
but most of all, thank you
just for being you.

YOU CAN CALL ON ME

Laura's car was totally unreliable.
But Laura's friend, Kelly, wasn't.
So when Laura's car broke down,
she called on Kelly.
"So, what's gone out this time?" Kelly asked.
"The brakes," Laura replied.
"Where are you?" Kelly asked.
"The pharmacy," Laura responded.
"And where's the car?" Kelly asked.
Laura sighed, "In here with me."

Friendship is the sheltering tree.
Samuel Taylor Coleridge

A true friend sees the first tear,
catches the second,
and stops the third.
Author Unknown

My life seems to have become
suddenly hollow, and I do not know
what is hanging over me.
I cannot even put the shadow
that has fallen over me into words.
At least into written words.
I would give a great deal
for a friend's voice.
John Addington Symonds

I felt it shelter to speak to you.
Emily Dickinson

Women draw strength from their friends.
When they need understanding
and somewhere to feel safe
and just be open, they know their friends are
waiting, with patience, kindness,
and a shoulder for them to cry on.

A good friend is the best medicine.
Proverb

Forget your woes when you see your friend.
Priscian

There is no physician like a true friend.
Author Unknown

A Friend Wants the Best for You, For Your Sake and Not Her Own

When something wonderful happens in the life of my friend, it just makes my day! Why? Because it is so satisfying to see that big, bright beautiful smile on the face of someone who is so loved and so deserving. Especially if life has been crummy lately and my friend needs cheering up and needs something like...getting a bouquet of flowers for no reason from someone who cares. Someone like me, for instance. Because, after all, that's what friends are for!

Friendship is the strong and habitual
inclination in two persons
to promote the good
and happiness of one another.
Eustace Budgell

True friends care about each other
with every fiber of their being,
and yet would never dream
of trying to own each other.
Author Unknown

My best friend is the person
who in wishing me well
wishes it for my sake.
Aristotle

If we would build on a sure
foundation in friendship,
we must love
friends for their sake rather
than for our own.
Charlotte Bronte

Friendship is thinking
of the other person first.
Author Unknown

I delight in my friend's joy...
and her heart rejoices in mine.

Friendship without self-interest
is one of the rare and
beautiful things of life.
James F. Byrnes

He does good to himself
who does good
to his friend.

Erasmus

That friendship will not continue
to the end which is begun for an end.

Francis Quarles

Dear Friend,
I give of myself to you
for the joy of seeing
your happiness.
That is what fills my heart
and brings me joy.
It is more than enough.

A Friend Is Someone Who Is Honest with Us

A FRIEND EVEN LOVES YOUR...

A friend not only knows all about you
and still likes you...
a friend thinks all your funny little
quirks and eccentricities not only
make you more interesting...
they make you charming, funny
and special and adorable
(Well...most of the time).

And a friend will tell you when you're
about to do something crazy
that you will regret later,
and will either talk you out of it

or volunteer to come along
and help you carry out your
risky business,
just to keep you safe or to make
you not feel all alone if you get caught.

And then your friend will NOT say
"I told you so" when she turns out
to have been right all along,
but will say "Well, I guess we both
learned something today"
and will then laugh with you about it.

A friend is better than a therapist,
your favorite shoes on sale,
a fresh bouquet of flowers,
and even chocolate...

Friends are a blessing for sure.

My true friends have always
given me that supreme proof
of devotion, a spontaneous
aversion for the man I loved.

Sidonie Gabrielle Colette

A good friend is someone
you can always count on,
to share with you,
laugh with you,
and tell you when you have
spinach in your teeth.

In friendship we find nothing
false or insincere;
everything is straight forward,
and springs from the heart.

Cicero

A friend is a person with
whom I may be sincere.
Before him I may think aloud.

Ralph Waldo Emerson

A friend will tell you when that new hair color
just isn't working, but she'll say
"That's nice but you looked so fantastic
in that other color".
And if you ask if that new pair of jeans
makes your back side look big,
she'll say "I think the cut on those pants
aren't doing justice to your cute figure."
You both know she's not being totally
straight with you
but it's because she loves you,
and you love her back for it.

Only friends will tell you
the truths you need to hear to make...
your life bearable.

Francine Du Plessix Gray

Only a real friend will tell you
when your face is dirty.

Proverb

The best thing we can find in our travels
is an honest friend.

Robert Louis Stevenson

A friend will tell you to stop texting
and pay attention to where you're driving!

But not TOO honest:

Though we should try to be entirely honest
with our friends, it is equally important that
we sometimes leave out those things
they simply don't need to know.

If we all told what we know of one another,
there would not be four friends in the world.

Blaise Pascal

WOMEN WORTH HANGING OUT WITH...

- assure you that you have an hourglass figure, even when the sands of time begin to shift.

- don't bat an eye when you order a side of chocolate chips with your salad.

- may witness you making a fool of yourself, yet don't believe it's a permanent condition.

Friends Nurture Each Other

The most I can do for my
friend is simply be his friend.
Henry David Thoreau

Friendship is a plant that
must often be watered.
Author Unknown

Those whom we support
hold us up in life.
Maria von Ebner Eshenbach

Wishing to be friends is quick work,
but friendship
is a slow ripening fruit.

Aristotle

If a man does not make new
acquaintances as he advances through life,
he will soon find himself left alone.
A man, Sir, should keep his friendship
in constant repair.

Samuel Johnson

I'd like to be the sort of friend
you have been to me.
I'd like to be the help that you've
been always glad to be.
I'd like to mean as much to you
each minute of the day,
As you have meant,
old friend of mine,
to me along the way.

Edgar A. Guest

To have a good friend is one of the highest delights of life; to be a good friend is one of the noblest and most difficult undertakings.

Author Unknown

Instead of loving your enemies, treat your friends a little better.

Ed Howe

Be courteous to all, but intimate with few, and let those few be well tried before you give them your confidence. True friendship is a plant of slow growth, and must undergo and withstand the shocks of adversity before it is entitled to the appellation.

George Washington

To keep up and improve Friendship,
thou must be willing
to receive a Kindness as well as do one.

Thomas Fuller

Actions, not words, are the true criterion
of the attachment of friends.

George Washington

One who knows how to show
and to accept kindness
will be a friend better than any possession.

Sophocles

There is nothing we like to see so
much as the gleam of pleasure in a person's eye
when he feels that we have sympathized with him,
understood him, interested ourselves in
his welfare. At these moments something fine
and spiritual passes between two friends.
These moments are the moments worth living.

Don Marquis

The hearts that never lean must fall.
Emily Dickinson

When we ultimately go home to God,
we are going to be judged on what we were
to each other, what we did for each other,
and especially, how much love we put in that.
It's not how much we give,
but how much love we put in the doing—
that's compassion in action.
Mother Teresa

A little word in kindness spoken,
A motion or a tear,
Has often healed the heart that's broken,
And made a friend sincere.
Daniel Clement Colesworthy

There was a definite process by which
one made people into friends,
and it involved talking to them and listening
to them for hours at a time.

Rebecca West

Go oft to the house of thy friend,
for weeds choke the unused path.

Ralph Waldo Emerson

Plant a seed of friendship;
harvest a bouquet of joy!

Author Unknown

A man cannot be said to succeed
in this life who
does not satisfy one friend.

Henry David Thoreau

Friends Make the Journey
Through Life Easier and More Fun

The road to a friend's house is never long.
Saying

Every journey is shorter
with a friend by your side.

On the road between the homes of friends,
grass does not grow.
Proverb

Friends are like a pleasant park
where you wish to go;
while you may enjoy the flowers,
you may not eat them.
Edgar Watson Howe

Friendship is honey, but don't eat it all.

Proverb

Friends make the world more beautiful,
the future more hopeful,
and "today" a lot more fun!

The company makes the feast.

Author Unknown

In reality, we are still children. We want to find
a playmate for our thoughts and feelings.

Dr. Wilhelm Stekel

But every road is rough to me
that has no friend to cheer it.

Elizabeth Shane

Every joke is twice as funny
when a friend is laughing at it
right along with you.

Friends Respect
Each Other's Differences

...one may be my very good Friend,
and yet not be
of my opinion.

Margaret Cavendish

I don't need a friend who changes
when I change and who nods when I nod;
my shadow does that much better.

Plutarch

We should behave to our friends
as we would wish
our friends to behave to us.

Aristotle

To respect each other's differences,
to agree to disagree
with love and understanding
in our hearts,
to cherish each other's individuality
as well as to enjoy all that you have in common
is the basis of long-lasting friendship.

The ideal friendship is to feel
as one while remaining two.

Sophie Swetchine

Many a person had held close,
throughout their entire lives, two friends that
always remained strange to one
another, because one of them
attracted by virtue of
similarity, the other by difference.

Emil Ludwig

We met by chance and became
friends on purpose. This happened, amazingly,
after we found we loved to talk to each other.
This was in spite of the fact that there probably
wasn't one thing we agreed upon! But your feelings
were so honest, your intelligence so sharp,
your attitude so respectful and your
expression so witty, that you made me
examine my own opinions to see if I really
did believe them. And then I couldn't
wait to see you again...so quickly and
enjoyably did the hours fly by.

Friends Touch Our Hearts

So many people cross our path as we travel through life. Some pass by in an instant and are never seen or thought of again. Others play a role for a while, then are gone. But every so often, we meet someone and there's a special connection, an understanding of one another, a feeling that we haven't just met... that instead, we've known each other for a very long time. And from that moment on, that person becomes a part of our lives, of our best moments and memories...and a part of our heart.

Sometimes someone reaches out
to touch our hand and ends up
touching our hearts forever.
Author Unknown

Friends See Life the Same Way

Are we not like the two
volumes of one book?
Marceline Desbordes-Valmore

To like and dislike the same things
can often serve as a foundation
for a lasting friendship.
Author Unknown

Similarity in outlook
creates friendship.
Democritus

Friendship is almost always
the union of a part of one mind
with the part of another;
people are friends in spots.
George Santayana

Madam, I have been looking
for a person who disliked gravy all my life.
Let us swear eternal friendship.

Sydney Smith

They discovered that they
both loved yellow, preferred cats
over dogs, liked their chocolate dark
and their heels flat, believed boyfriends
were not always dependable
but girlfriends were, and then they
promised to be friends forever.

Friendship is a union of spirits,
a marriage of hearts,
and the bond there of virtue.

Samuel Johnson

True friends...
face in the same direction, toward common
projects, interests, goals.

C. S. Lewis

Friends Increase Our Joy
And Lessen Our Sorrows

SHE'S THERE FOR YOU

When troubles are piling up
and life is getting you down
and, instead of a sunny smile,
you're wearing a great big frown,
A friend is the first to notice
and it gives her heart a tug.
She'll throw her arm wide open
and give you a big warm hug.

And when you feel under the weather
and are stuck for days in bed,
she'll come over to make you soup and tea
when she could be somewhere else instead.
A friend is there when you need her
and doesn't care what others may say.
She's better than a chocolate sundae
or an umbrella on a rainy day.

Friends feel each other's joys
and sorrows as their own.

Author Unknown

She's always there to listen,
share your heart, or lend a hand.
She makes you laugh and helps
you cry as only a true friend can.

True happiness arises, in the first place,
from the enjoyment of oneself,
and in the next, from the friendship
and conversation of a few select companions.

Joseph Addison

I count myself in nothing else
so happy As in a soul remembering
my good friends.

William Shakespeare

Happy is the house that shelters a friend.

Ralph Waldo Emerson

Shared joy is double joy,
and shared sorrow is half-sorrow.

Proverb

"I'm so happy for you,"
are the most beautiful
words in the world,
coming from someone
who sincerely means it.

Friends Treat Each Other with Respect

THE REFLECTION OF ANGELS

"You're an angel!" We hear these words, and many may say them ourselves, as an expression of thanks and appreciation. It's true—some acts of kindness and generosity come at just the right time and seem heaven-sent.

The work of angels to bless our lives inspires us to bless the lives of others. We reflect angelic goodness when our thoughtfulness touches hearts, and when our help lightens the burdens of others. When we protect the vulnerable and encourage the weak, we are truly acting like angels.

Who has been like an angel in your life? And who are those who look at you and perceive the face, hands, and heart of an angel.

Don't walk behind me.
I may not lead.
Don't walk in front of me.
I may not follow.
Just walk beside me
and be my friend.

Albert Camus

No distance of place or lapse
of time can lessen the friendship
of those who are thoroughly
persuaded of each other's worth.

Robert Southey

I hold this to be the highest task
for a bond between two people;
that each protects the
solitude of the other.

Rainer Maria Rilke

A friend gives you total
freedom to be yourself.

Author Unknown

Friends Make Life Better

Close friends are truly life's treasure.
Sometimes they know us better than
we know ourselves. With gentle honesty,
they are there to guide and support
us, to share our laughter and our tears.
Their presence reminds us that
we are never really alone.

Vincent Van Gogh

I'm so thankful for friendship.
It beautifies life so much.

L. M. Montgomery

The world is so empty if one thinks
only of mountains, rivers and cities;
but to know someone thinks and feels
with us, and who, though distant,
is close to us in spirit,
this makes of the earth for us
an inhabited garden.

Johann Wolfgang von Goethe

The feeling of friendship is like being
comfortably full of your favorite dessert
and discovering it had no calories.

Friends warm the heart,
lift the spirit,
and bless your life.

A friendship like love is warm;
a love like friendship is steady.

Thomas Moore

A cheerful friend is like a sunny day,
which sheds its
brightness on all around.

John Lubbock

It was such a joy to see thee.
I wish I could tell how much thee is to my life.
I always turn to thee as a sort of rest.

Lady Henry Somerset

Good friends, good books
and a sleepy conscience:
this is the ideal life.

Mark Twain

A friend is one of the best things to have…
and to be.

Author Unknown

True friends are the people who say
nice things about us behind our backs.

Author Unknown

Friendship isn't a big thing
it's a million little things.

Author Unknown

Friendship is the sweetener of life.

Saying

Let us be grateful to people
who make us happy;
they are the charming gardeners
who make our souls blossom.

Marcel Proust

We know from daily life that we
exist for other people first of all,
on whose smiles and well-being
our own happiness depends.

Albert Einstein

The better part of one's life
consists of his friendships.

Abraham Lincoln

A friend is a present you give to yourself.

Robert Louis Stevenson

There is no happiness like that of being
loved by your fellow creatures,
and feeling that your presence is an
addition to their comfort.

Charlotte Bronte

But in Friendship—in that luminous,
tranquil, rational world of relationships freely chosen...
this alone, of all the loves, seemed to raise you
to the level...of angels.

C. S. Lewis

Human beings are born into
this little span of life of which the best thing
is its friendships and intimacies....

William James

"If I had a flower for every time I thought of you...
I could walk through my garden forever."

Alfred Lord Tennyson

Friends Help Us through the Hard (and not so hard) Times

So closely interwoven
have been our lives, our purposes,
and experiences, that, separated,
we have a feeling of incompleteness—
united, such strength of self-assertion
that no ordinary obstacles,
differences or dangers ever
appear to us insurmountable.

Elizabeth Cady Stanton

Friends lift us up when the rest of the
world lets us down.

Friends can see
what's invisible to the eye
because they look with the heart.

You know a real friend?
Someone who will look after
your cat when you're gone.

Author Unknown

When the going gets rough,
your fair weather friends get going,
but your true friends stay right
by your side.

Loyalty is what we seek in friendship.

Cicero

I should like to tell you again
of my bitter troubles so that mutually,
by recounting our grief,
we can lighten each other's sorrow.

The Kanteletar

Friendship is certainly the finest balm
for the pangs of disappointed love.

Jane Austen

A friend will give you an umbrella
when it's raining,
offer you a shoulder when
you need one to
cry on, hold your head
when you're sick, tell you
a joke to cheer you up when
you're sad, and split her
last piece of chocolate with you.

New Friends Enrich Our Lives

SO NICE TO MEET YOU!

We've all been in the situation where we find ourselves at a party or some kind of event, and we don't know one single solitary soul there. We smile, we look around for a familiar face, get up the courage to introduce ourselves to a few strangers, and start watching the clock, planning a graceful and unobtrusive escape.

And then, we overhear a witty comment by someone nearby, and we laugh. Our eyes meet and we realize we have something in common. Or maybe she's wearing the absolute most gorgeous necklace we've ever seen so we compliment her, and she says "I made it myself" and "I was just admiring yours!" And suddenly the evening takes on a whole new aura of fun and excitement, the time flies by, we exchange phone numbers…and before we know it, we're having lunch, meeting each other's kids, making plans together... and feeling like we've known each other forever.

I never enter a company without
the hope that I may discover a friend,
perhaps the friend, sitting there with
an expectant smile. That hope survives
a thousand disappointments.

Arthur Christopher Benson

A new friend is always a miracle.

Henry Adams

Friendship is born at that moment
when one person says to another:
What! You too? I thought I was the only one.

C. S. Lewis

Old friends grow older along
with us and help us on the journey through
life and all its changes, but new friends inspire
us to think new thoughts and look
at life in new ways and that helps us to stay young.

Yes'm, old friends is always best,
'less you can catch a new one that's fit
to make an old one out of.

Sarah Orne Jewett

Since there is nothing so
well worth having as friends,
never lose the chance to make them.

Francesco Guicciardini

New friends can often have
a better time together than old friends.

F. Scott Fitzgerald

A new friend can often give you
a whole new way of looking at life,
or introduce you to a new interest...
or even help you to look at yourself in a new way,
because they see something in you
that you didn't even know was there.
New friends can be full of surprises
and adventures that you didn't even know
you were looking for!

At unexpected moments...
God places an angel in our path—
Someone we will soon call "friend."

Friends Are a Treasure

But friendship is the breathing rose,
with sweets in every fold.

Oliver Wendell Holmes

Friendship is the golden thread that
ties the heart of the world.

Author Unknown

I awoke this morning with devout
thanksgiving for my friends, the old and the new.

Ralph Waldo Emerson

Think where man's glory most begins
and ends, and say my glory
was I had such friends.

William Butler Yeats

It is a good thing to be rich,
it is a good thing to strong,
but it is a better thing to be beloved
of many friends.

Euripedes

I have friends in overalls whose
friendship I would not swap for the
favor of the kings of the world.

Thomas A. Edison

Words are easy, like wind.
Faithful friends are hard to find.

William Shakespeare

All love that has not friendship
for its base, is like a mansion
built upon the sand.
Ella Wheeler Wilcox

Hold a true friend
with both your hands.
Proverb

Thine own friend,
and thy father's friend,
forsake not.
Proverbs 27:10

The best way to keep
your friends is not to give
them away.
Wilson Mizner

Treasured times and treasured friends
are blessings of the heart.

Friendship is Love
without his wings.
Lord Byron

Your wealth is where
your friends are.
Plautus

May I a small house and large garden have,
and a few friends,
and many books, both true.
Abraham Cowley

To the world you may only be one person,
but to one person you may be the world.

Author Unknown

A big house doesn't keep you from
feeling lonely inside it. Lots of money
in the bank doesn't call you
when you're feeling sad. Diamonds don't tell
you funny stories because they love to make you
laugh and see you smile.
Your stock portfolio won't come to your
funeral and tell the world what a great person you were
and how much you'll be missed.
Let's face it...friends are just a lot more fun
than a bunch of stuff, and without them,
there just wouldn't be much point to anything else.

Friendship doesn't make
the world go 'round.
Friendship is what makes
the ride worthwhile.

Author Unknown

Friends Are Family

THE BEST KIND OF FAMILY

When we think of "family", certain characteristics and expectations come to mind. Your family is where your home is, where you're loved unconditionally, supported whole-heartedly, valued, respected, treated with tenderness and caring, welcomed in with affection, understood, encouraged, and, in general, even liked.

Certain old sayings also come to mind. A favorite one is "Home is where they have to take you in." Truth is, there are those sad situations in life where one's Home bears little resemblance to the above description.

But all is not lost...not even close! This old world is filled with millions of wonderful loving people. And amongst those millions, just waiting to be discovered so they can accept, love and welcome us into their lives are our future friends...our spiritual family...our own people.

And what's so beautiful about it is that they need us as much as we need them! And like us, they've been searching for and waiting for us their entire lives so they can form a real family as well—a family they, too, have chosen...a family not related by blood but by love...a family of the heart.

Chance makes our parents,
but choice makes our friends.
Author Unknown

Secret to a happy life:
Treat your friends like family
and your family like friends!

A sympathetic friend can be quite
as dear as a sister.
Author Unknown

Ruth to Naomi, her mother-in-law:
Whither thou goest, I will go;
and where thou lodgest,
I will lodge:
thy people shall be my people,
and thy God my God.

Ruth 1:16

A good friend is my nearest relation.
Thomas Fuller

There's a point in every true friendship,
when friends stop being friends
and become sisters.
Author Unknown

One loyal friend is worth
ten thousand relatives.
Euripides

Sometimes God makes two women friends,
because if they were sisters their mom
couldn't have handled it.
Author Unknown

Friends are family you choose for yourself.
Author Unknown

Friends Grow Old Together
(well, maybe just a little older...)

REMEMBERING TOGETHER

Old friends aren't just
the people we share memories with...
they're the people who were there
at the very moment
when the memories were made.

They remember having
the same kindergarten teacher,
and playing on the swings at recess
and being chased around the playground
by rough little boys with dirty faces
whom we gave nicknames.

Or maybe we met in middle school,
those awkward years of first pimples
and growing spurts,
and they remember the first time

we wore mascara or got braces
or had a crush on one of those
rough little boys who grew up
actually to be pretty cute.

Maybe our old friend was there
for our driving test,
arguments with our parents,
high school graduation,
our first summer job.

I recently spent some time with a friend
I've known since third grade.
She was my best friend all through school,
and my maid of honor when I got married.

I remember her long red braids
when I met her,
her scary older brother,
her intelligence and great sense of humor,
what a great cook her mom was.
Her mom is gone now, but her brother
remains and is a lot less scary.
She's as smart and funny as ever.

Now we're near retirement age…
and what a lovely, enjoyable time we had,
laughing about our teenage angst
and antics,
about situations we got into
that we never did tell our parents about,
about mutual old friends we still remember
and even hear from every once in a while.

Old friends take us back
to when we were young,
and they remind us of how much
we've grown and experienced.
They reflect back to us
how much older and wiser
we really have become,
and they give life a kind of continuity
and meaning that puts things
into perspective and helps us see
what's really important…
that it's the relationships in our lives
that really matter,
did then, do now, and always will.

There is no friend like an old friend
who has shared our morning days,
no greeting like his welcome,
no homage like his praise.

Oliver Wendell Holmes

Friendship is the shadow
of the evening, which
increases with the setting sun of life.

Jean de La Fontaine

There is no better treasure
than a good friend, except a good friend
who grows to be an old friend.

Should auld acquaintance be forgot
and never brought to mind?

Robert Burns

To me, fair friend, you can never be old.

William Shakespeare

Old friends are the great blessing
of one's later years....
They have a memory of the same
events and have the same
mode of thinking.

Horace Walpole

...the companions of our childhood
always possess a certain power over
our minds which hardly any
later friend can obtain.

Mary Shelley

We've been friends since we
were just young sprouts—
and we'll still be friends
when we're older than dirt.

The best mirror is an old friend.
Author Unknown

Ah, how good it feels!
The hand of an old friend.
Henry Wadsworth Longfellow

May the hinges of our
friendship never grow rusty.
Blessing

It is great to have friends
when one is young, but indeed it is still
more so when you are getting old.
When we are young, friends are,
like everything else, a matter of course.
In the old days we know
what it means to have them.

Edvard Grieg

As we grow older, we don't lose friends.
We just find out who the real ones are.

Author Unknown

One of the nice things about
old friends is that they never think
you look any older because
they've been growing older right
alongside of you. They don't think
you're any more forgetful
than they are, so of course,
you're absolutely normal.
And they don't think
you have any more
wrinkles or sags than they do
because you don't.

True friends don't change
with the changing times.
They just have fun sitting around talking
about how things used to be back
when they were oh-so-slightly younger.

Friends Touch Our Hearts

Oh, the comfort—the inexpressible comfort
of feeling safe with a person—
having neither to weigh thoughts nor
measure words, but pouring them
all right out, just as they are, chaff and
grain together; certain that a faithful hand
will take and sift them, keep what is
worth keeping, and then with the breath
of kindness blow the rest away.

Dinah Mulock Craik

A friend is a person who listens
attentively while you say nothing.

Author Unknown

A friend doesn't care if your house is messy,
but compliments you on the flowers in your garden.

A loyal friend laughs at your jokes
when they're not so good,
and sympathizes with your problems
when they're not so bad.

Author Unknown

We may not be perfect,
but we're perfect for each other!
Friends don't have to feel like
they're perfect to feel accepted.
They just feel loved for being so
perfectly themselves!

If you judge people,
you have no time to love them.

Mother Teresa

A friend should bear his friend's infirmities.

William Shakespeare

The best rule of friendship is to keep your
heart a little softer than your head.

Author Unknown

A True Friend Is Irreplaceable

THERE'S ONLY ONE YOU

Most of us have perhaps one person we can tell everything to...only one, rarely more. Why only one? There are so many reasons we choose that one person, but it begins with trust. We have to feel we can confide anything, our hopes, our fears, our mistakes, with complete faith that our privacy and our feelings will be respected and protected.

We need to know that we will be listened to with unselfish interest, with compassion and understanding, and sometimes, even forgiveness.

And it helps to know that we can share all this without being judged, that our friend will still love us and be on our side in spite of our shortcomings.

We are drawn to this friend because we feel exactly the same way about her and treasure her feelings and her trust as a wonderful gift we have been blessed to receive.

And, of course, there is the fun side to it— the sharing of the good things in both our lives and the knowledge that our friend finds joy in seeing us happy and takes pleasure in sharing a smile.

This kind of friend is rare, a true blessing in our lives. No one is like her, for she is unique and wonderful and much loved.

We wish she could live forever because there will never be anyone like her.

She is irreplaceable.

'Tis the human touch in the world that counts,
the touch of your hand and mine,
Which means far more to the fainting heart
than shelter and bread and wine. For shelter is gone
when the night is o'er, and bread lasts only a day.
But the touch of the hand and the sound of the
voice sing on in the soul always.

Spencer M. Free

SHE CAME FOR ME

She didn't bring me flowers,
or a loaf of home-made bread,
She wasn't dressed for going out to tea.
She didn't bring a fancy gift or
books that she had read,
But she stayed and we watched re-runs on TV.

She came as quickly as she could,
with heart of purest gold
And had no expectations I could see,
But she brought the biggest treasure that my
heart could ever hold...
What I needed most was her. She came for me.

A TRUE FRIEND
is someone who...

... remembers your birthday,
   but forgets your age.

... says nice things about you
   behind your back.

... will take your call, even if
   she's busy.

... only keeps a secret from you when
   she's planning your surprise party.

... knows everything about you,
   but loves you anyway.

There comes a point in your life
when you realize who really matters,
who never did, and who always will.

Author Unknown

Truly great friends are hard to find,
difficult to leave,
and impossible to forget.

Author Unknown

Greater love hath no man than this,
that a man lay down
his life for his friends.

John 15:13

A true friend becomes a part of you.
She has a place in your heart and a role
in your life. She becomes your counselor,
adviser, playmate, confidante, partner in crime,
fashion consultant, chauffeur sometimes,
workmate, luncheon companion, recipe
swapper, secret keeper and all-around buddy.
And when she's gone, there's a huge space left
behind because of all the ways she filled your life.
And it never goes away. So all you can do is fill
that space that gratitude that she was in your life,
comfort yourself with all the great memories you
made together, and think about how great it will
be to see her again some day...and start making
a list of all the things you'll want to tell her about.
Because you just know she'll say "Tell me all,
and don't leave a thing out!"

Friends Reflect Who We Are

A good friend is like a mirror,
reflecting back to you
the very best of who you are.

Tell me whom you frequent,
and I will tell you
who you are.

Proverb

He that walketh with wise men shall be wise.

Proverbs 13:20

Life is partly what we make it,
and partly what it is made
by the friends we choose.

Tehyi Hsieh

Since birds of a feather
flock together,
it's a good idea to hang out
with people whose values you respect,
because the people that you meet
in the course of your life
will just assume you spend your time
with people you have the most in common with.
If you share your life with kind and caring people,
it will rub off on you.

When making a new friend,
decide whom you admire
and would like to be more like
and see if the feeling
is mutual.

Friends Give Us the Benefit of the Doubt

Thank you,
Dear Friend, for supporting me,
even when you think I might be wrong.
And thank you for then very gently and lovingly
telling me in private why you suspect
there might be just a tiny wee chance
that I should reconsider my position.
I hear you, I respect your opinion,
and I feel the love in your honesty
and your kindness.

A friend is one who withholds
judgment no matter how long
you have his unanswered letter.

Sophie Irene Loeb

Who seeks a faultless friend
remains friendless.

Proverb

Two persons cannot long be
friends if they cannot
forgive each other's little failings.

Jean de La Bruyere

The proper office of a friend
is to side with you when you are
in the wrong. Nearly anybody will side
with you when you are in the right.

Mark Twain

I like a Highland friend who
will not stand by me only when
I am in the right, but when I am
a little in the wrong.

Sir Walter Scott

We shall never have friends
if we expect to find
them without fault.

Author Unknown

Never explain.
Your friends do not need it
and your enemies will not
believe you anyway.

Elbert Hubbard

Friends Are Kind to Each Other

We cannot tell the precise moment
when friendship is formed. As in filling a vessel
drop by drop, there is at last
a drop which makes it run over. So in a series
of kindnesses there is, at last, one which
makes the heart run over.

James Boswell

There is nothing better than
a kind word of encouragement
from a good friend.

Author Unknown

Give and take makes good friends.

Proverb

Friendship requires great communication.

Francis de Sales

There isn't much that I can do,
But I can sit an hour with you,
And I can share a joke with you,
And sometimes share reverses, too…
As on our way we go.

Maude V. Preston

Kind words can be short
and easy to speak,
but their echoes are truly endless.

Mother Teresa

Many a friendship—
long, loyal, and self-sacrificing—
rested at first upon no thicker
a foundation than a kind word.

Frederick W. Faber

There is nothing I would not do
for those who are really my friends.
I have no notion of loving people by halves,
it is not my nature.

Jane Austen

Do good to thy friend to keep him.

Benjamin Franklin

The rule of friendship means
there should be mutual sympathy between them,
each supplying what the other lacks
and trying to benefit the other,
always using friendly and sincere words.

Cicero

Friends for Life

Friendship at first sight,
like love at first sight,
is said to be the only truth.
Herman Melville

Perhaps the most delightful friendships
are those in which there is much agreement,
much disputation,
and yet more personal liking.
George Eliot

I suppose there is one friend
in the life of each of us who seems not
a separate person, however dear
and beloved, but an expansion,
an interpretation, of one's self.
Edith Wharton

True friendship comes when silence between
two people is comfortable.

Author Unknown

Some of the best conversations
between friends are in moments
of silent understanding.

It's the folks that depend on us for this and for
the other that we most do miss.

Mary Webb

It is not time or opportunity that
is to determine intimacy;—
it is disposition alone.
Seven years would be insufficient
to make some people acquainted
with each other, and seven days
are more than enough for others.

Jane Austen

There are people we meet in
life that make everything
seem magical. Cherish them.

Author Unknown

Good friends are those who
care without hesitation,
remember with limitation,
and love even without
communication.

Author Unknown

A true friend is someone who
calls me when I'm in the middle of
texting her because we thought of each
other at the same time.

I am learning to live close to
the lives of my friends without ever seeing them.
No miles of any measurement
can separate your soul from mine.

John Muir

No friendship is an accident.

O. Henry

There are no rules for friendship.
It must be left to itself.
We cannot force it any more than love.

William Hazlitt

Friends Are Chosen with Care

Remember, you don't need a
certain number of friends,
just a number of friends you can be certain of.

Author Unknown

Be slow to fall into friendship;
but when thou art in,
continue firm and constant.

Socrates

Have but few friends,
though many acquaintances.

Author Unknown

Books and friends
should be few but good.

Author Unknown

Be slow in choosing a friend,
slower in changing.

Benjamin Franklin

Friends should be like books,
few, but hand-selected.

C. J. Langenhoven

Friends Look Out for Each Other

A friend won't let you laugh,
drive and put on
mascara at the same time.

If someone is saying mean
things about you to your friend,
they will not only disagree with everything
that person says, they will give them
a hard glassy stare that will freeze
them in their shoes.

When it hurts to look back
and you're afraid to look ahead,
you can always look beside you
and your best friend will be there.

Author Unknown

The sincere friends
of this world are as ship lights
in the stormiest of nights.

Giotto de Bondone

Life has no blessing
like a prudent friend.

Euripides

MISSED YOU TODAY

Thought of a funny story today,
one that would catch you by surprise
and make you smile
and then laugh uproariously,
and missed you
because you weren't around to
share it with me.

Finished a really good book today
that was so interesting and moving
and well-written that I knew
the characters would resonate with you
and that you would love it, too,
and missed you
because you weren't here
to discuss it with me.

Heard about a great new restaurant today
that specializes in some of your
favorite dishes
and has a great garden patio
for us to enjoy,
and missed you
because you weren't in town
to make a reservation with me.

Heard some news today
that made me feel sad
and wonder what the world
is coming to, for goodness sake,
and missed you
because you weren't here to listen,
and to give me your views,
which always make me feel better
about the world.

Counted in my head
all the things about you
that make me love you,
my dear friend,
so very much,
and missed you
because you weren't here
so I could sit on the porch
and, over tea, tell you personally
about each and every one.

Sweet is the memory of distant friends!
Like the mellow rays of the departing sun,
it falls tenderly,
yet sadly, on the heart.

Washington Irving

The pain of parting
is nothing to the joy of meeting again.

Charles Dickens

Friends Laugh Together

A friend will make you laugh so hard
that your soda will come out your nose,
and then will give you her last tissue
to clean up your face.

Laughter is not a bad beginning for a
friendship, and it is far the best ending for one.
Henry Ward Beecher

Good friends don't let friends
do stupid things...alone.
Author Unknown

A friend is someone who picks you up when
you fall down, makes sure you're okay, and
then laughs with you about how silly you looked.

A friend tickles our funny bone
and touches our heart.

Which of all my important nothings
shall I tell you first?
Jane Austen

Laugh and the world laughs with you.
Cry and you're forced to dig out
that used fast food napkin from
the bottom of your purse.

Friends who can laugh together,
last together.

Among those whom I like or admire,
I can find no common denominator,
but among those whom I love, I can:
all of them make me laugh.
W. H. Auden

A Friend Is Always the First to Come When Needed

Friendship is like the immortality of the soul,
is too good to be believed. When friendships
are real, they are not glass threads or frost work
but the solidest thing we know.

Ralph Waldo Emerson

"Watson. Come at once if convenient.
If inconvenient, come all the same."

Arthur Conan Doyle

Friends are always together in spirit.

L. M. Montgomery

When you're sick, a friend will come over,
fluff up your pillows, make you a cup of tea,
and bring you up to date on all the latest news.

When a friend is in trouble,
don't annoy him by asking
if there is anything you can do.
Think up something appropriate and do it.

E. W. Howe

Before you can even call her,
a friend is at your door.

Love is like the wild rose-briar;
Friendship is like the holly-tree—
The holly is dark when
the rose-briar blooms,
But which will bloom most constantly?

Emily Bronte

A faithful friend is a strong defense;
And he that hath found him
hath found a treasure.

Louisa May Alcott

Friendship is like a tree whose roots live
deep in the earth, but whose limbs reach
up to heaven, ready to catch you when you
feel you're about to fall.

Friends Enjoy Our Company

I want someone to sit beside after
the day's pursuit and all its anguish,
after its listenings, its waitings, and its suspicions.
After quarreling and reconciliation, I need privacy—
to be alone with you, to set this hubbub in order.
For I am as neat as a cat in my habits.

Virginia Woolf

Somehow desserts just seem to taste better
when a friend is across the table,
sharing it with you
as you discuss each other's day.

And last but not least....

THE TOP FIFTEEN REASONS
FRIENDS ARE BETTER THAN CHOCOLATE

1. Friends don't go straight to your hips.
2. They're not on sale to anyone with a buck.
3. They melt your heart, but they don't melt all over your favorite white blouse.
4. They're neither too sweet or too bitter, too big or too small; friends are just right!
5. If you don't see them for a long time, they're not all dried up and waxy when you see them again.
6. Friends raise your spirits but not your cholesterol.
7. You know they're really listening to you instead of just sitting there like a lump.
8. When they're nutty they make you laugh, and you don't have to pick them out of your teeth later.
9. You don't have to worry if they're real or just some new fake substitute.
10. Friends don't make your face break out (except in smiles).
11. You don't have to feel guilty for spending too much time with them.
12. They don't make you pass out from a sugar coma if you have too many.
13. You already know what's inside of them and that it's something you love.
14. The best ones aren't the most expensive.
15. And friends make life better, not just for a moment, but forever!